The Lost City of
Machu Picchu

Rob Waring, *Series Editor*

NATIONAL
GEOGRAPHIC
LEARNING

Australia · Brazil · Mexico · Singapore · United Kingdom · United States

Words to Know

This story is set in Peru, South America. It happens at a place called Machu Picchu [mɑtʃu piktʃu], in the Andes mountain range.

A **Machu Picchu and the Ancient World.** Read the paragraph. Complete the definitions with the underlined words.

Machu Picchu was an <u>ancient</u> city in the Andes Mountains. A group of people called the Inca built Machu Picchu a long time ago. The Inca <u>civilization</u> lasted from around A.D. 1100 until about A.D. 1500. When it suddenly ended, few people knew about Machu Picchu. Because of this, it is sometimes called the 'Lost City of the Incas.' In 1911, an American <u>explorer</u> found Machu Picchu. Since then, many people have visited Machu Picchu to <u>climb</u> the <u>ruins</u> of the city.

1. move up or over something: _____
2. very old: _____
3. a person who travels to learn about new places: _____
4. the remains of buildings: _____
5. people and culture: _____

mountains

Inca man

Inca woman

The Lost City of Machu Picchu

B. Machu Picchu and the Modern World. Read the paragraph and notice the underlined words. Then answer the questions.

The <u>modern</u> world, or the world of today, has now come to Machu Picchu. A big part of this modern world is <u>tourism</u>. Tourism is a business that brings visitors to a place. These visitors, or <u>tourists</u>, come from many countries. Some <u>conservationists</u> think tourism might be bad for the environment. They want to protect Machu Picchu. They don't want a lot of tourists to go there.

1. Why do you think tourists want to go to modern day Machu Picchu? List three or more reasons.
2. Why do you think conservationists are worried about Machu Picchu? List three or more reasons.
3. What do you think will happen to Machu Picchu in the future? How can people protect it?

Tourists in Modern Day Machu Picchu

This beautiful, quiet place is covered in sunshine and has very high mountains all around it. Its name is Machu Picchu. It's sometimes called the 'Lost City of the Inca', and it's nearly **8,000 feet**[1] up in the Andes Mountains of Peru.

The story of Machu Picchu is the story of a place where the ancient world and the modern world meet.

---

[1]**8,000 feet:** 2,438 meters

 CD 2, Track 01

Julio is a **tour guide**[2] and he knows Machu Picchu very well. He thinks that it has a special quality. It has something which brings people to it. "It's a magic attraction that you can feel here," he explains. "It's known all over the world that Machu Picchu is one of the **magnetic centers**[3] of the ancient world," he says.

---

[2]**tour guide:** a person who shows visitors around and gives them information about a place

[3]**magnetic center:** a special area which pulls energy towards it

Machu Picchu is a city with a long history; it's more than 500 years old. Today, it's a favorite place for visitors. These visitors are not only people from Peru. People from all over the world go to Machu Picchu. They want to attempt to step back in time and to understand the Inca civilization. They don't only go there in the sunshine, either. Even in the **fog**,[4] many think it's wonderful to climb up the mountain and walk through the ruins of the city.

---

[4]**fog:** a cloud near the ground that makes it difficult to see

Scan for Information

Scan page 8 to find the information.

1. How old is Machu Picchu?

2. Who visits Machu Picchu?

3. What is one thing visitors do there?

When the Inca civilization ended, few people knew that Machu Picchu ever existed. For a long time Machu Picchu was lost to the outside world. Then, in 1911, an explorer named Hiram Bingham found it again.

At first, very few people visited the ruins of Machu Picchu. But now, hundreds of tourists come here every day. They walk up the steps of the ancient city and climb over the ruins. Machu Picchu is no longer quiet. It's currently full of the sounds of visitors. And not everyone likes it. Some people want the tourists to come, but other people don't.

Hiram Bingham

Some people in Peru hope that even more tourists will come to Machu Picchu. They think it will mean more business and money for the country. These people want to make it easier for tourists to get to Machu Picchu. They also want to establish better, more modern, tourist services. They say that tourism will improve things for Peru and its people.

However, some conservationists worry that more visitors won't be good for Machu Picchu. They say that tourism may not be good for the environment or for the old ruins. Others worry that the ancient city will change. They worry that it will lose its special quality. They think it may become just like any other place.

One man, however, is not worried about this at all. José owns a local hotel. He says that Machu Picchu and Peru need more visitors. The 'Lost City' is a very special place, he claims, and everyone should be able to see it. "Why not be like the rest of the world?" he says. "Why not **expose**[5] and show Machu Picchu to the rest of the world?" He then adds, "It's such a wonderful place, why keep it to a few?"

It's obvious that some people, like José, support tourism, and some people are against it. So what does tourism mean to Peru? The truth is that parts of Peru are very poor. The tourist trade brings a lot of money to some communities.

---

[5]**expose:** let people see

Infer Meaning

1. What's the purpose of José's comment?
2. How does José feel about tourism in Machu Picchu?

Aguas Calientes[6] is a good example of a tourist community. Aguas Calientes is a town that is in the area where visitors get on buses to go to the **summit**[7] of Machu Picchu. Because of this, it grew suddenly and went from nothing into a town.

Aguas Calientes has no industry except tourism. The town is just a group of **stalls**.[8] The local people here sell art and other things they have created to the visitors. The people there live completely on money from tourists. It's their only income.

_____

[6]**Aguas Calientes:** [ɑgwɑs kɑlyɛnteɪs]
[7]**summit:** top of a mountain
[8]**stall:** a small shop with an open front or a table

What is happening to the special quality and beauty of Machu Picchu today? Tourism is certainly changing the area. But are the effects good or bad? No one can decide.

However, one thing is certain: Time may be running out for the 'Lost City of the Inca.' This 'Lost City' is no longer lost. Tourists have found it and the modern world is coming closer to this ancient world every day. In the end, it may be the modern world that forever changes this ancient society.

---

[9]**time may be running out:** there might not be much time left

After You Read

1. On page 5, the word 'beautiful' can be replaced by:
    A. sunny
    B. lovely
    C. dark
    D. hot

2. What is a good heading for page 6?
    A. People Don't Know About Machu Picchu
    B. The Magical Energy of Machu Picchu
    C. Machu Picchu Is Known All Over the Ancient World
    D. Julio Talks About the Incas

3. Machu Picchu is a city with _____ long history.
    A. the
    B. many
    C. a
    D. some

4. On page 10, 'they' in paragraph two refers to:
    A. tour guides
    B. Incas
    C. tourists
    D. explorers

5. How many visitors come to Machu Picchu every day?
    A. a few
    B. one
    C. none
    D. hundreds

6. How do conservationists feel about tourism in Macchu Picchu?
    A. If too many tourists come, the lost city will change.
    B. Many people should come to Machu Picchu.
    C. Machu Picchu is not very beautiful for tourists.
    D. The world is not interested in the lost city.

7. How does the hotel owner feel about tourism in Machu Picchu?
   A. If too many tourists come, the lost city will change.
   B. Many people should come to see Machu Picchu.
   C. Machu Picchu is not very beautiful for tourists.
   D. The world is not interested in the lost city.

8. Tourism brings _____ money to Peru.
   A. more
   B. no
   C. a
   D. the

9. On page 17, the phrase 'local people' on paragraph two means:
   A. tourists in the town
   B. people from far away
   C. people from Aguas Caliente
   D. conservationists at Machu Picchu

10. On page 18, what is 'it' in 'tourists have found it'?
   A. the modern world
   B. the special quality
   C. the ancient history
   D. the lost city

11. A good heading for page 18 is:
   A. Modern World May Bring End to Ancient City
   B. Little Time to Become a Modern City
   C. A Lot of Time Left for Machu Picchu
   D. A Modern Machu Picchu Is Better

TWO VIEWS OF MACHU PICCHU

The TELT Times recently received two letters to the government office of tourism in Peru. One is in favor of increased tourism in the area around Machu Picchu. The other letter is against allowing large numbers of tourists to visit the ruins. You decide who's right.

Greater International Understanding

I think Peru should do everything it can to bring more tourists to Machu Picchu. People from other countries will pay a lot to visit this beautiful and historic site. I live near Machu Picchu and strongly believe this money will help the local people have a better life. Visitors from other countries also provide a way for people to share their cultures. As a result, this will lead to greater international understanding. Bringing more attention to the area will also help people realize that it's important to keep the ruins in good condition.

Yours truly,
Richard Wellner
SBC Tours Incorporated

Not a Pleasant Experience

Recently, I visited Machu Picchu. As I reached the summit, the fog cleared and suddenly I saw the view! The mountains were so beautiful. Then our tour guide showed us some of the 200 ancient buildings. We walked around for hours enjoying the views and looking at the buildings. It is a very special place.

However, the experience was not a totally pleasant one. I'm concerned that too many people are visiting the area. For one thing, it was impossible for us to find a quiet place to sit and enjoy the view. People were running everywhere. Secondly, I could see that the large numbers of tourists are starting to have a bad effect on the land. People have cut down a lot of the trees. They also leave paper and other things they do not want on the ground. Some of the ancient stones have even been moved or broken. I think the government should make laws limiting the number of tourists who can visit Machu Picchu each year.

Yours truly,
Martha Gorman
Concerned Community Member

CD 2, Track 02

Word Count: 338
Time: _____

Vocabulary List

ancient (2, 5, 6, 10, 12, 13, 18)
civilization (2, 8, 10)
climb (2, 8, 10)
conservationist (3, 13)
explorer (2, 10)
expose (14)
fog (8)
magnetic center (6)
modern (3, 5, 13, 18)
ruins (2, 8, 10, 13)
stall (17)
summit (17)
time may be running out (18)
tour guide (6)
tourism (3, 14, 17, 18)
tourist (3, 10, 13, 14, 17, 18)